CIPS Study Matters

Level 6

Graduate Diploma in Purchasing and Supply

PASSNOTES

Leading and Influencing in Purchasing

© Profex Publishing Limited, 2010

Printed and distributed by the Chartered Institute of Purchasing & Supply

Easton House, Easton on the Hill, Stamford, Lincolnshire PE9 3NZ

Tel: +44 (0) 1780 756 777

Fax: +44 (0) 1780 751 610

Email: info@cips.org

Website: www.cips.org

First edition October 2006
Second edition August 2007
Third edition April 2009
Reprinted with minor amendments October 2010

Contents

Preface

Welcome to your **Passnotes!**

This element of your Study Pack has been specially designed to support you in your exam revision.

- Small-format **Passnotes** fit easily into a bag or briefcase: **convenient to use** wherever and whenever you have a few minutes for topic review or exam revision.

- The material is organised in **short, clearly labelled units**: easy to work through systematically or to dip into at any point, if that's what you prefer.

- Each area of the unit content starts with a simple **mind-map** of the relevant Learning Objectives, helpfully **cross-referenced** to chapters in your Course Book (so you can quickly locate more substantial topic coverage, if you need to refresh your memory).

- The units cover each (and all) of the **Learning Objectives** in turn (again, cross-referenced to other units where topics overlap), so you can see exactly what knowledge and understanding underpins potential exam questions.

- Within each unit, the material is presented in a format specially designed for **ease and speed of learning** – essential in the revision stage of your studies! **Passnotes** use key definitions, point lists, action plans, tables and diagrams:

  - To keep the topic coverage as focused and brief as possible
  - To offer an easily grasped overview of each topic
  - To make the topic more visual – and therefore (for most people) more readily memorable.

- For relevant topics, we also include Integrated Learning Checklists: point lists and action plans gathered from different Learning Objectives to give you a broader handle on topics, processes and management challenges. (Particularly useful for case study questions...)

Of course, Passnotes don't give you substantial or comprehensive coverage of the unit content. (That's what your **Course Book** is for.) What they do give you is **systematic and focused coverage**: a concise, easy-to-remember survey of the key points on which you can base an exam answer. This makes them ideal to use in the weeks and days leading up to the exam!

And don't forget: updates, case studies, advice on exam technique and other revision-support resources (including practice questions with full solutions) will be regularly added to the study resources.

Good luck.

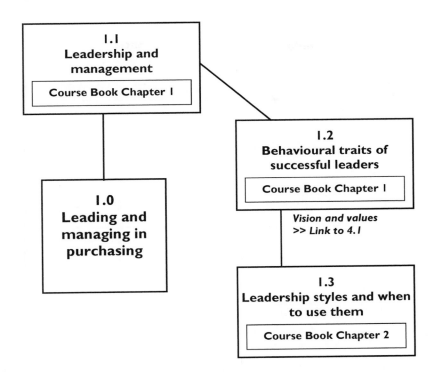

Management is 'the process through which efforts of members of the organisation are co-ordinated, directed and guided towards the achievement of organisational goals'.
Leadership is 'a relationship through which one person influences the behaviour or actions of other people'. *(Mullins)*

Management v leadership

Management...	Leadership...
Is about coping with complexity: applying structure, control > order, continuity	Is about coping with change: creating direction, vision, energy/inspiration
Can be exercised over process, projects, resources, time (ie mainly organisational)	Can only be exercised over people (ie mainly interpersonal)
Is based on a formal role and position in the organisation (> subordinates)	Is based on the perception and choice of others (> followers)
Aims to secure compliance for standard levels of performance	Aims to secure willingness/commitment for extra performance, flexibility, loyalty etc
Is about organising to achieve stated purposes	Is about finding direction in the face of critical challenges

NB: 'Managers cannot be successful without being good leaders, and leaders cannot be successful without being good managers' *(Whetten & Cameron)*.

Leaders are in demand because they:

☑ Energise and support **change**
☑ Secure **commitment** and **input** from employees (>> innovation, improved service)
☑ Set **direction** (>> co-ordinated team-working and guided empowerment)
☑ Develop **people** (>> maximised contribution)
☑ **Facilitate and empower** (>> flexibility, innovation, employee satisfaction/loyalty)

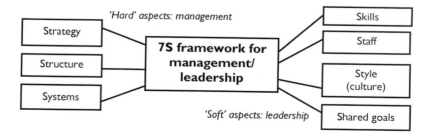

What leaders really do

Managerial roles (*Mintzberg*)		
Management work, in practice, is disjointed, discontinuous, informal, intuitive and interpersonal. It is best thought of not as discrete actions but as shifting roles.		
Interpersonal	**Informational**	**Decisional**
• Figurehead • Leader • Liaison	• Monitor • Spokesperson • Disseminator	• Entrepreneur • Disturbance handler • Resource allocator • Negotiator

Action-centred leadership (*Adair*)		
Leadership is a process which takes place in a context made up of three basic objectives		
Achieving the task	**Developing/satisfying individual group members**	**Building/maintaining an effectively functioning group**

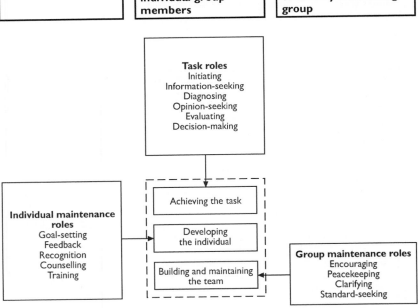

Task roles
Initiating
Information-seeking
Diagnosing
Opinion-seeking
Evaluating
Decision-making

Individual maintenance roles
Goal-setting
Feedback
Recognition
Counselling
Training

Achieving the task

Developing the individual

Building and maintaining the team

Group maintenance roles
Encouraging
Peacekeeping
Clarifying
Standard-seeking

Challenge-focused approach (*Pedler, Burgoyne, Boydell*)		
Leadership is defined 'by what we actually do when faced with challenging situations. Leadership is principally concerned with recognising, mobilising and taking action in the face of critical problems and issues.'		
Challenges: critical tasks, problems and issues against which resources need to be mobilised, action taken.	**Characteristics:** qualities, competencies and skills that individuals can bring to bear on the challenge situation.	**Context:** immediate conditions operating in the challenge situation. ('What works here and now may not work in another place and at another time'.)

Leadership roles in purchasing

Head of purchasing (or chief purchasing officer)	<ul><li>Overall responsibility for work of purchasing function</li><li>Strategic leadership in areas such as policy development</li><li>Represents the function in dealings with other departments: stakeholder management, interpersonal, communication skills</li></ul>
Senior purchasing manager	<ul><li>Leader/co-ordinator of team of purchasing managers (or cross-functional Purchasing Council)</li><li>Within strategy framework, responsible for broad decisions on market evaluation, sourcing, appraisal/selection of suppliers, negotiations with suppliers, award of contracts</li><li>May be responsible for single category of purchase</li></ul>
Purchasing manager (or category manager)	<ul><li>Similar in scope to senior purchasing manager, at lower level</li><li>Large organisations: a team, each responsible for a category</li><li>Role typically ends with award of contract</li></ul>
Purchasing leadership team	Team comprising senior members of purchasing function, led by HoP: co-ordination/communication mechanism: meetings focus on strategic direction > flow down to purchasing staff.
Purchasing team leaders	Contracts Manager, Supplies Manager, Project Managers with responsibility for particular areas, leading teams/sections etc.

Purchasing and supply strategy formulation and alignment

Integrating purchasing activity within the organisation and supply chain

Securing stakeholder buy-in to plans, initiatives, projects

Leadership focus in purchasing

Ethical leadership (via input to environmental, sustainability, CSR goals)

Establishing and applying meaningful Key Performance Indicators (KPIs) for purchasing activity

Network leadership (directing multi-functional teams, creating supply chain partnerships)

Leadership traits

Trait theories suggested that certain personality characteristics (traits) 'make' good leaders, but no verifiable list of traits could be agreed.

Adaptability to situations	Decisiveness	Persistence
Alertness to social environment	Dependability	Self-confidence
Ambition and achievement orientation	Dominance (willingness to influence others)	Willingness to assume responsibility
Assertive communication	Tolerance of stress	Co-operation
	Energy	

>> Focus on how leaders *behave:*

- Leadership styles (**>> Unit 1.3**)
- Leadership skills and values

Leadership skills and values

Vision
- Vision = 'a desired future state of the organisation'
- Putting in place a picture of a compelling future: involving others, focusing on achievement, keeping it fresh and relevant

Emotional intelligence (EQ)
- 'The capacity for recognising our own feelings and those of others, for motivating ourselves, and for managing emotions well in ourselves as well as in others' *(Goleman)*

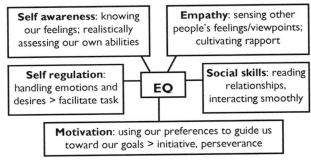

- EQ underpins leadership qualities eg confidence, perseverance, flexibility, tolerance of stress
- Social skills underpin inspiring, persuading, motivating, leading, negotiation, teamworking etc.
- EQ for change management: supports transformational approach (changing underlying beliefs/values)

Values and integrity
- Values are things we attach importance to
- 'Guiding values' > inspire, control behaviour *(>> Unit 4.1)*
- Integrity: consistency, openness, honesty, respect for people, ethical standards

Inter-personal skills

Second-order skills
Negotiation; influencing and persuading; teamworking; managing conflict; managing people through change; coaching/facilitating; leading

First-order skills
Observing; active listening; purposeful questioning; establishing rapport; expressing empathy; communicating assertively; giving and receiving feedback

- **Promotion:**
  - ❏ Selling visions/goals/values to others (AIDA: Attention, Interest, Desire, Action)
  - ❏ Self-promotion (image or impression management)

- **Influencing and persuasion:**
  - ❏ Applying 'pressure' (eg authority, power) to change other people's attitudes or behaviours
  - ❏ Persuasion: influencing *other* than by authority/power (eg by logical argument or emotional appeal)   *(>> Unit 2.1)*

- **Inspiration:** expressing powerful values/vision > arouse follower aspirations; modelling attractive values/behaviours > induce follower emulation

- **Support and challenge:** *Support* (coaching, encouragement, empathy) > confidence, security + *Challenge* (goal articulation, feedback, questions, targets) > learning, stretching, change

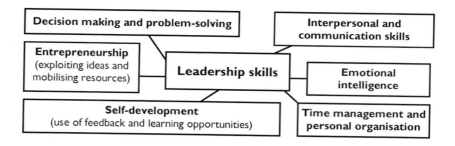

Leadership style is 'the way in which the functions of leadership are carried out; the way in which the manager typically behaves towards members of the group'. *(Mullins)*

Style theories describe and categorise behavioural preferences or styles of managers, usually on a continuum *(Tannenbaum & Schmidt)* between:

Wholly task focused/
Directive behaviour

Wholly people focused/
Supportive behaviour

Autocratic ← → Democratic

Managerial control

Subordinate discretion

Directive behaviours	Facilitative/supportive behaviours
Letting group know what is expected	Jointly agreeing objectives/standards
Giving specific guidance/instructions	Delegating responsibility for day-to-day
Asking group to follow rules/procedures	Offering guidance/info if required
Scheduling/co-ordinating work plans	Championing the team
Monitoring/controlling performance	Giving helpful feedback (critical friend)
Suitable where:	*Suitable where:*
• Group does not share objectives	• Group is willing, able and confident
• Group lacks ability or confidence	• Group input/acceptance is important
• Time is short and results critical	• Task/problem is relatively unstructured
• Group is willing to accept authority	• Culture supports participation

Autocratic style	Democratic style	Laissez-faire style
Power centralised in hands of leader: communication and interaction focus on or through leader: leader > command/control role	Decision-making shared by team via participation processes; wider group interactions; leader > facilitate/empower role	Team autonomous; organises own work, makes decisions (within objectives/budget etc): leader > coaching role

Task v people focus: Blake & Mouton's managerial grid

Two-dimensional model of leadership styles based on concern for task/production mapped against concern for people.

Tool of leadership development: identify lack of balance; identify how manager may modify style > more effective.

(9, 9) assumed to be 'ideal' style but eg (9, 1) autocratic style may be effective in crisis or authoritarian cultures...

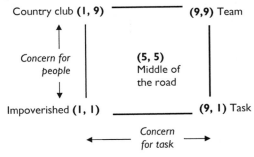

Country club (1, 9) ——————— (9,9) Team

Concern for people

(5, 5) Middle of the road

Impoverished (1, 1) ——————— (9, 1) Task

Concern for task

7

Managerial assumptions: McGregor's Theory X and Theory Y

'Every managerial act rests on assumptions, generalisations and hypotheses': Theory X and Y are *not* 'types of people', but extreme managerial assumptions *about* people.

Theory X	Theory Y
People dislike work and seek to avoid it They must be coerced, controlled, directed or bribed/threatened to work They prefer security to responsibility	Work is natural and can be satisfying People exercise self-direction and self-control if committed to objectives, and are willing, if encouraged, to seek responsibility
>> Directive/autocratic/controlling style	>> Participative/facilitative style

Range of styles: the Ashridge studies (tells, sells, consults, joins)

Tells (*autocratic*)	**Sells** (*persuasive*)	**Consults** (*participative*)	**Joins** (*democratic*)
Leader makes decisions, issues instructions.	Leader persuades team to accept decisions.	Leader takes team input into account in making decisions.	Leader seeks team consensus for decisions.
☑ Fast decisions ☑ Efficient for programmed, automated work ☒ Discourages input, feedback and initiative	☑ More commitment, understanding ☒ Still one-way, not much input, initiative	☑ Better quality and commitment through input ☑ > upward communication ☒ Takes longer	☑ Empowerment ☑ Commitment ☑ Quality input ☒ May undermine authority ☒ Takes longer ☒ 'Political' decisions

Transactional v transformational leadership *(Burns)*

- **Transactional leaders**: relationship with followers seen in terms of mutual dependence and trade: give rewards in exchange for service/compliance.

  Effective in stable organisations (eg bureaucracies) with security-seeking, authoritarian cultures, operating in stable, slow-change environments.

- **Transformational leaders**: role seen as stimulating interest, raising awareness, motivating and inspiring >> change cultures and create new direction.

  Effective in dynamic, fast-changing and competitive environments; lean, flexible organisation structures (eg networks, virtual teams) and innovative/learning cultures.

Idealised influence: win respect, trust and emulation by acting as role model for team values	**Inspirational motivation**: express value of goals/contribution, compelling future, high expectations, confidence
Intellectual stimulation: support learning, creative problem solving, questioning, innovation, stretching	**Individualised consideration**: treat people as individuals; listen, support individual development; celebrate diversity

Situational approach

'Leaders need to interact with their team in different ways in different situations.' (*Gillen*)

- **Action centred leadership** (*Adair*): most appropriate action depends on relative priority of task needs, individual needs and group needs. >> **Unit 1.1.**

- **Situational leadership** (*Hersey & Blanchard*): most appropriate style depends on follower maturity/readiness level (willingness, ability, confidence).

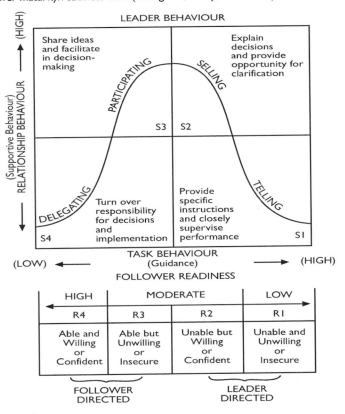

Evaluating contingency/situational approaches:

☑ Emphasise need for leader flexibility
☑ Encourage self-awareness > emotional intelligence
☑ Provide basis for developing leaders

☒ May be seen as manipulative, unless handled with integrity
☒ May create leader inconsistency > stressful for subordinates
☒ Requires intuition re variables (hard to measure in practice)

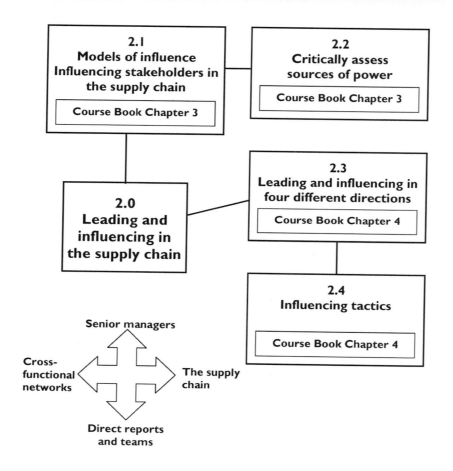

Collaboration, adversarialism and accommodation

Thomas: model of relationship styles in conflicts of interest:

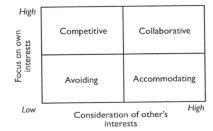

- **Avoiding**: you withdraw from conflict: attempt to sweep under the carpet.

- **Competing (adversarialism)**: you impose your solution on the problem. In supply chain: arm's length communication; competitive negotiation; lack of trust; little info sharing; individual transactions, tight controls; maximising own share of benefits.

- **Accommodating**: you concede the issue without a fight, to preserve harmony (eg if highly dependent on relationship, or in poor bargaining position).

- **Collaborating**: both parties work to find 'win-win' to clearly stated needs. In supply chain: working together to add value (via quality, development, info exchange, operational linkage, shared definition of norms/expectations, relationship-specific adaptations to products/processes) + sharing of added value > mutual benefit.

[**NB**: adversarial competitive relationship: collaboration at operational level to increase value – but competition at commercial level to appropriate as much of value as possible.]

Influencing

Influencing is the process of applying some form of pressure in order to change other people's attitudes or behaviours: to secure their compliance, obedience, conformity or commitment.

Influencing – *not* negotiation
Not a single event: continual process
Not necessarily intentional/conscious
Need not involve two-way discussion
Need not end with explicit agreement
Need not involve compromise

Influencing – *not* manipulation
Positive influencing: non-manipulative, persuading behaviours that demonstrate you are treating people openly, honestly and respectfully >> use of active listening, empathy, rapport, persuasion, assertiveness

PUSH approach
Exerting power or authority
Influencees fully aware of the process
Aim: to secure compliance
Result: mere compliance, often resentment

PULL approach
Persuasion or interpersonal influence
Influencees may not be consciously aware
Aim: to secure commitment/ownership
Result: positive, trusting relationship, collaboration

Rapport

Rapport is the sense of relationship or connection we have when we relate to other people. We have 'positive rapport' with people we find warm, attentive and easy to talk to: we feel comfortable and relaxed with them.

☑ Helps establish openness and trust
☑ Supports influencing through pacing and leading (establishing empathy/trust before reframing/changing); creating trust/liking; overcoming barriers

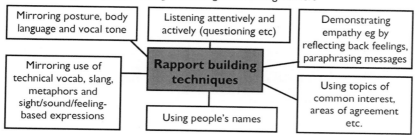

| Mirroring posture, body language and vocal tone | Listening attentively and actively (questioning etc) | Demonstrating empathy eg by reflecting back feelings, paraphrasing messages |

Rapport building techniques

| Mirroring use of technical vocab, slang, metaphors and sight/sound/feeling-based expressions | Using people's names | Using topics of common interest, areas of agreement etc. |

Trust

Scholtes: trust depends on a combination of competence/capability (your ability to do what someone asks of you) and care (your sensitivity to their needs).

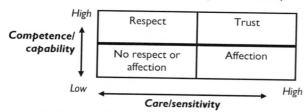

	High	Respect	Trust
Competence/ capability ↕		No respect or affection	Affection
	Low		

Care/sensitivity — Low ←→ High

Persuasion

Persuasion pulls or leads people to change by bringing their beliefs and goals into alignment with those of the influencer.

❑ **Logical argument**: each step of the argument clearly explained and linked; demonstration of objectivity, fairness to both sides of argument; support from relevant and verifiable factual info.

❑ **Facilitative techniques** (helping the 'penny drop' for others): question-and-answer; summarising; getting feedback (checking understanding); flexible responses

❑ **Persuasive communication style**: rapport; open body language; pacing and leading; speaking with appropriate emphasis, appeal and interest.

❑ **Persuasive strategy**: appealing to needs, goals and interests of the influencee: offering benefits, motivators (positive and negative reinforcement).

Stakeholder mapping: power and dependency issues

Stakeholders are groups who have an actual or potential 'stake' in the activity of an organisation (interest), or who impact on it in some way (influence).

NB Stakeholder/organisational objectives may **coincide** (eg supplier gives reliable, cost-effective supply >> organisation gives supplier ongoing profitable business) but may not!

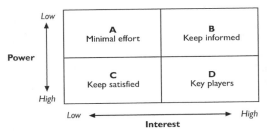

Power/Interest Matrix *(Mendelow):* map stakeholder influence and likelihood of getting involved >> identify appropriate strategy for communication/engagement.

Kraljic matrix ('procurement positioning' tool): determine power/ dependency issues of particular purchased items.

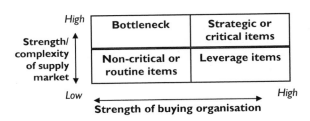

Power/dependency matrix *(Cox et al):* determine dependency within supply relationships.

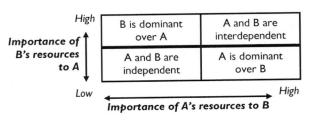

If these diagrams don't ring a bell in detail: see Chapter 4 of your Course Book.

Models, strategies and tactics of influence: **>> Unit 2.4**

Influencing external stakeholders: **>> Unit 2.3**

Power

Power is the ability to exert influence over objects, persons or situations. It may or may not be formally conferred in an organisation in the form of legitimate authority.

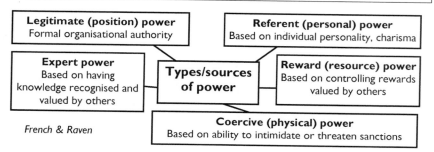

Legitimate (position) power
Formal organisational authority

Referent (personal) power
Based on individual personality, charisma

Expert power
Based on having knowledge recognised and valued by others

Types/sources of power

Reward (resource) power
Based on controlling rewards valued by others

French & Raven

Coercive (physical) power
Based on ability to intimidate or threaten sanctions

A purchasing manager has legitimate power (within own function); expert power within the organisation (eg to set purchasing policy or advise on negotiations); resource power within the supply chain (through awarding contracts); and perhaps personal power (through rapport with individual supplier representatives).

❑ **Legitimate power**: purchasing officials have direct line authority over the members and activities of their department, section or team. (**>> Unit 1.1**)

❑ **Expert power**:

- Staff authority: expert power of a specialist giving advice or guidance to another manager or department.

- Functional authority: expert given legitimate authority to direct the activities of line managers and departments in the area of his or her expertise (eg centralised purchasing on behalf of user departments, or imposing tendering procedures, standard forms etc for users).

- Potential source of political issues: perception of undermining line authority; 'ivory tower' advice; territorial expansion by red tape etc >> need for scope/limits to be clearly defined; mutual line/expert respect fostered; purchasing demonstrate awareness of strategic/operational objectives of internal customers.

❑ **Reward power**:

- Over purchasing staff: control over pay and benefits, praise, promotion prospects, development opportunities, info etc.

- Over suppliers: control over contracts, recognition etc. (Power stronger if supplier dependent on buyer for major proportion of income; difficult for supplier to attract other buyers; buyer perceived to have direct control over decision.)

❑ **Reference power**: via inspirational role modelling, persuasive influencing, trust/rapport in relationships etc.

❑ **Coercive power**: generally dysfunctional in business, because only secures compliance (often with resistance, resentment, potential for broken relationship).

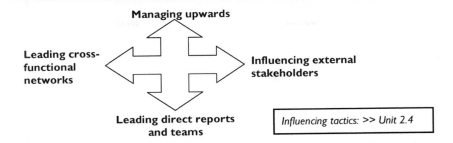

Managing upwards

Leading cross-functional networks

Influencing external stakeholders

Leading direct reports and teams

Influencing tactics: >> Unit 2.4

Managing upwards

☑ Lower levels of management gain access to authority, info and resources
☑ People gain support/authorisation to put plans into action
☑ Follow-through on promises of support/resources maximised
☑ Expectations of superiors managed > realistic deadlines, resources etc
☑ Superiors habituated to exception reporting > avoid micro-management
☑ Achievements of individuals/teams promoted > recognition of ability/potential
☑ Emergent ideas find shape/direction through communication, evaluation and lobbying
☑ Models upward communication > encourage suggestions/feedback from own team

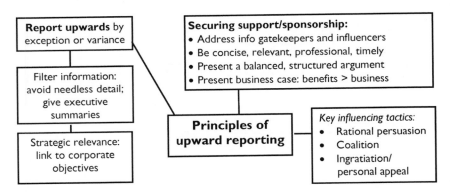

Report upwards by exception or variance

Filter information: avoid needless detail; give executive summaries

Strategic relevance: link to corporate objectives

Securing support/sponsorship:
• Address info gatekeepers and influencers
• Be concise, relevant, professional, timely
• Present a balanced, structured argument
• Present business case: benefits > business

Principles of upward reporting

Key influencing tactics:
• Rational persuasion
• Coalition
• Ingratiation/personal appeal

Leading direct reports and teams

Key influencing tactics:

• Inspirational appeal (by transformational/democratic leaders)
• Rational persuasion (> secure buy in)
• Pressure (by autocratic leaders)
• Consultation (in wider employee relations context)

See also leadership behaviours and styles: >> *Units 1.1– 1.4*

Cross-functional leadership

Issues for lateral influence:

- May not be supported by legitimate position power (**>> Unit 2.2**)
- May involve relative equality of power, interdependency
- May involve inter-functional, line/staff political conflict

Key influencing tactics:

- Personal appeal/ingratiation
- Rational persuasion
- Exchange (likelihood of genuine reciprocity)
- Legitimating (to depersonalise power issues)
- Networking > 'connection power' *(Pedler et al)*
- Interdepartmental promotion, profile-raising and image/issues management *(Taylor)*

Reasons for increase in cross-functional teamworking:

- ❑ Increasing involvement of purchasing staff in strategic procurement decisions
- ❑ Increasing adoption of supply chain philosophy > need for integrated work flow
- ❑ Makes best use of developments in ICT
- ❑ World class systems (eg MRP, TQM) require teamwork for implementation
- ❑ Global market/technology development etc > need for expert input

> - ☑ Reduction in time to get things done (via co-ordinated effort)
> - ☑ Improved ability to solve complex problems
> - ☑ Improvement in organisation's customer focus
> - ☑ Improved creativity, innovation, learning (via multi-disciplinary interaction)

> Short-term project work or longer-term programmes: eg global sourcing, outsourcing, new product development, quality management, purchase of capital items etc.

Programme owner/sponsor	Sets objectives, takes overall responsibility for achievement (eg HoP)
Steering committee	Senior managers from user/stakeholder functions, chaired by HoP. Advice and support for programme/project
Programme manager	Responsible for operational matters, deadlines, standards

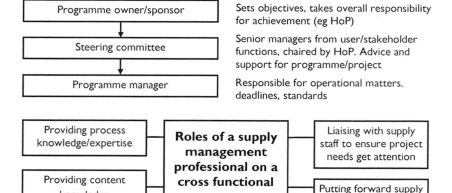

External stakeholders

Stakeholder	Interest (stake)	Influence/power
Managers/ employees	Survival/growth of employer Task/personal goals	Formal authority Control over resource/skills
Shareholders	Financial performance of firm	Voting rights, ownership
Customers	Satisfaction of expectations Safe products, ethical dealings	Power to boycott/switch Legal remedies
Suppliers & distributors	Reliable revenue stream Information/feedback support Mutually beneficial relationship	Control strategic resources Expertise (eg subcontractor) Strategy implementation
Government and agencies	Economic activity, tax revenue Reports and returns	Power to legislate/regulate Strategy (eg public sector)
Interest groups	Awareness of cause/issues Protection of rights	Power to lobby, boycott, generate publicity
Professional bodies/unions	Protection of rights of members Promoting standards/ethics	Control over members Advisory/consultative
Community/ wider society	Employment and amenities Provision of goods/services Social responsibility	Influence government policy Potential customers Control over resources

The first three rows (Managers/employees through Suppliers & distributors) are marked **Connected**. The last four rows (Government and agencies through Community/wider society) are marked **External**.

Flow diagram:
Identify stakeholder groups → Assess stakeholder power/influence / Assess stakeholder interest *(Mendelow matrix)* → Map stakeholder management strategies → Assess key stakeholder goals → Stakeholder planning: how to negotiate mutual goal fulfilment?

Why manage stakeholder expectations?

- Gain expert input to plans
- Easier collaboration ('ownership' and support for agreed plans)
- Mobilise power and resources

- Plan to minimise resistance
- ❑ **Stakeholder mapping:** >> *Unit 2.1*
- ❑ **Stakeholder marketing:** What messages? What benefits can be promoted?
- ❑ **Relationship management**: Communication? Supporter engagement/motivation?
- ❑ **Issues management:** How to raise potential issues/problems? What consultation/ involvement to minimise impacts/resistance?
- ❑ **Danger signals:** What behaviours/responses might indicate resistance or lack of commitment?

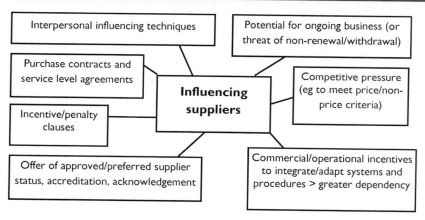

Key influencing tactics:

- Exchange (but NB: commercial relationship of mutual benefit: not personal inducements to influence decisions!)
- Consultation (especially in collaborative/partnership relationships)

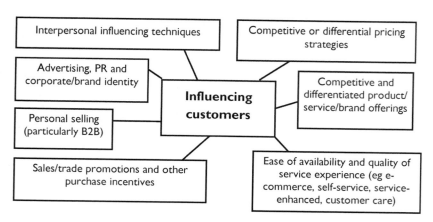

Key influencing tactics:

- Rational persuasion (eg product/price comparison)
- Inspirational appeal (value-laden branding)
- Consultation (seeking customer feedback)
- Ingratiation (relationship marketing)
- Exchange (sales promotions)

Impression (image) management	**Political influence**	**Proactive influence**
Create or enhance your credibility and congeniality in the eyes of other people.	Gain and apply various forms of power, to influence decisions in favour of your interests.	Create conditions in which you're more likely to get what you want: rapport, trust etc.

Influencing tactics (Yukl & Falbe)

Tactic	Approach
Rational persuasion	Logical argument and evidence, designed to demonstrate credibly that the request or plan is desirable and feasible.
Inspirational appeal	Appeal to the influencee's ideals, values, aspirations, and/or statements of encouragement/belief > confidence/enthusiasm.
Consultation	Asking influencees to participate in planning, or demonstrating willingness to take their ideas/concerns into account. Often used where input would enhance a decision, or acceptance would enhance its implementation.
Ingratiation	Getting the influencee to think well of you, or to be in a co-operative frame of mind, before a request is made.
Exchange	Offering reciprocal exchange of favours or promising a share of the benefits or added value accruing from the plan.
Personal appeal	Appealing to personal friendship and loyalty.
Coalition	Seeking help of others to persuade influencee, or using the fact of their support as a reason for the influencee to agree as well.
Legitimating	Establishing the legitimacy of a request by demonstrating one's right to make it: eg based on positional authority, compliance with rules, policies or practices etc.
Pressure	Threatening sanctions, or using assertiveness bordering on aggression, to demand compliance or 'wear down' resistance.

Escalation: raising of intensity of response to situation (level of adversarialism; intensity of pressures applied; move from pull to push; appeal to higher authority).

☑ Shows you're serious; wears down resistance; minimises frivolous objections
☒ Costs; potential for hardened resistance, resentment, reciprocal obligations etc.

Nature of relationship: >> Unit 2.3

Leader's power/resources to make tactic work

Acceptability of the tactic within the culture

Choice of tactic

Likely response (v goals)

Ethicality of the tactic and its consequences for others

Potential costs of the tactic (reciprocal obligations, loss of credibility etc)

Resistance: intended influencees position themselves against the request and actively attempt to avoid having to comply with it.

Symptoms of resistance:

- Outright refusal (if the influencer lacks power) or objections (to dissuade)
- Apathy or excuses (avoiding involvement)
- Requests for change or clarification (causing delay)
- Undermining the influencer or plan (eg by foot-dragging, sabotage, criticism, creating opposing coalition, appealing to higher authority)
- Grudging compliance (without commitment or initiative)

☒ Undermines project and leader's authority

☒ Results in grudging compliance at best: at worst, conflict and sabotage

☑ Can clarify issues; highlight genuine problems; stimulate problem-solving, consultation and consensus (for better quality decision and greater commitment later)

Compliance: intended influencees are willing to do what is requested – but no more: they make the minimal effort necessary to satisfy the terms of the legal/psychological contract. Underlying attitudes have not been altered.

Symptoms of compliance:

- Doing only/exactly what is 'required': work to rule, minimal standards
- Grudging attitude: no enthusiasm or creativity

☑ May be sufficient: eg where work is highly programmed or automated.

☑ May be necessary/positive: eg in sense of compliance with legal/regulatory requirements. (Even then: 'the law is a floor' > seek good/best practice.)

☒ No commitment, imagination, initiative, flexibility necessary for: complex/flexible processes; focus on service/knowledge, relationship management, quality, innovation.

Internalisation (or **commitment**) is where intended influencees are brought to agree internally with the request, decision or viewpoint: it is aligned with their own goals/beliefs, so that they are able to buy into it in a personally committed way.

Symptoms of internalisation/commitment:

- Willingness to put forth extra effort/energy at own initiative
- Proactive input/ideas/suggestions for innovation or improvement
- Willingness to collaborate to resolve conflicts and problems constructively
- Willingness to work independently of supervision/controls
- Communication/teaching of values/ideas to others

☑ Long-lasting, stable change in attitudes and behaviour

☑ Harnessing effort/energy/creativity

☑ Basis of mutually-beneficial, long-term relationships and exchanges

---

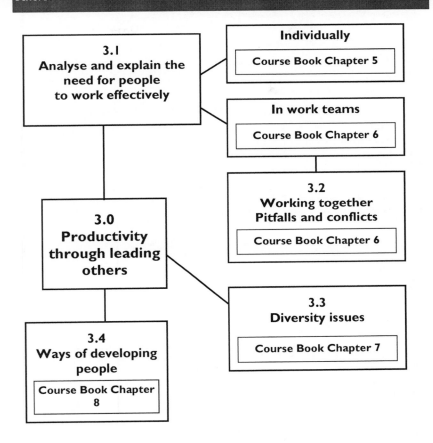

Why productivity through people?

☐ People add value to material, financial, informational and other resources

☐ People factors (knowledge, service, relationships) are key to competitive advantage

☐ People are not just a cost to be controlled, but an asset to be nurtured and developed to maximise their contribution

FACTORS IN INDIVIDUAL PERFORMANCE

Commitment	Contribution	Capability
How willingly people approach their work and add value for the organisation: • Motivation (see below) • Leadership	Conditions to support effective working: • Commissioned • Controlled • Championed • Co-operative	Sourcing and development of: • Capacity • Competence • Creativity

Personality

Personality comprises the psychological qualities that influence an individual's characteristic behaviour patterns, in a distinctive and consistent manner across different situations and over time.

eg   The Myers-Briggs Type Indicator (MBTI®) model:

Extrovert (E): energy outwards	Introvert (I) : energy inwards
• Sociable and expressive • Impulsive • Learn through practical/'hands-on'	• Private and reserved • Controlled or inhibited • Learn through reflection
Sensing (S): concrete sensory info	**Intuitive (N) : mental processes**
• Observe physical details of events • Learn through practical application • Place trust in experience	• Observe patterns and insights • Learn through ideas and theories • Place trust in insight and hunches
Thinking (T) : evaluating facts	**Feeling (F) : identifying with people**
• Guided by reason, explanation • Make decisions with heads • Aspire to be 'reasonable'	• Guided by values and impacts on people • Make decisions with hearts • Aspire to be 'compassionate'
Judging (J) : meaning/conclusions	**Perceiving (P) : taking in information**
• Prefer to be organised, methodical • Structure: detailed plans, schedules • Like certainty, achievement, closure	• Prefer to be flexible, casual, spontaneous • Keep options open • Like ambiguity, uncertainty, change

☐ Allow for differences in working styles, without judging them (no style/type is 'best')

☐ Adapt your behaviour to others' to build rapport and influence

☐ Utilise the strengths of each type and the way they complement each other in a team

Learning

> **Learning** is the 'relatively permanent change in behaviour that occurs as a result of practice or experience'. (*Bass & Vaughan*)

❑ **Behaviourist psychology**: learning is the formulation of new connections between stimuli (sensory experiences) and responses, on the basis of experience or 'conditioning' >> importance of application/practice, feedback, incentives (positive reinforcement) and deterrents (negative reinforcement).

❑ **Cognitive psychology**: learning is how we use feedback info on results of past behaviour to make rational decisions about what to do in future >> importance of clear goals, feedback, incentives/motivation.

❑ **Learning cycle** (*Kolb*): tool for turning everyday work experience > learning.

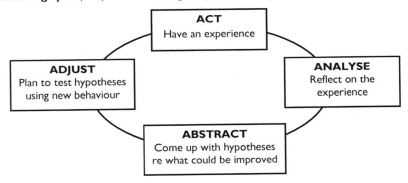

❑ **Learning style preferences** (*Honey & Mumford*):

Theorists	Reflectors	Activists	Pragmatists
Need to understand underlying concepts prior to hands-on	Need to observe/ research and reflect before acting	Need to work on practical tasks or problems	Need to see direct link to real task or problem
Prefer structured, theory-based training programmes	Prefer own-pace, info-rich training programmes	Prefer hands-on, participative training programmes	Prefer on-the-job, applied training programmes
Strong at 'Abstract' stage of cycle	Strong at 'Analyse' stage of cycle	Strong at 'Adjust' stage of cycle	Strong at 'Act' stage of cycle

Leader/developer can:

- Include elements which will suit learner's preferred/strong style
- Include elements to stretch/develop learner's less-preferred/weak style
- Include elements which will suit all four learning styles (for group learning)

Training and development: >> *Unit 3.4*

Motivation

> **Motivation** is the mental process by which people choose desired outcomes and decide how to go about them *and* the social process by which one party can influence these decisions in others (eg via rewards and incentives).

Some major motivation theories:

- **Hierarchy of needs** *(Maslow)*. People behave in a way that satisfies a need or drive: when a basic need (eg for security and social belonging) is satisfied, they move on to higher needs (eg for recognition and personal growth).

  > Management task: offer rewards/incentives that satisfy needs.

- **Two-factor theory** *(Herzberg)*. The need to avoid unpleasantness is satisfied by *hygiene* factors in the environment (eg pay, conditions, leadership style, company administration). The need for personal growth is satisfied by *motivator* factors in the job itself (eg challenge, interest, learning, responsibility, recognition, achievement).

  > Management task: control hygiene factors (to minimise dissatisfaction) and offer motivator factors (for positive performance).

- **Expectancy theory** *(Vroom)*. Force of motivation depends on the individual's strength of preference for a given outcome/reward (valence) and his belief that he will get that outcome/reward (expectancy).

  > Management task: set clear goals, give performance feedback, offer rewards valued by people and be consistent in following through with offered rewards.

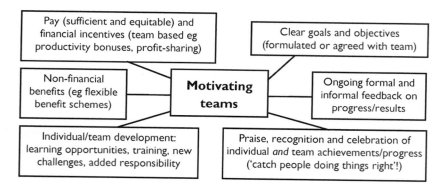

- Pay (sufficient and equitable) and financial incentives (team based eg productivity bonuses, profit-sharing)
- Clear goals and objectives (formulated or agreed with team)
- Non-financial benefits (eg flexible benefit schemes)

Motivating teams

- Ongoing formal and informal feedback on progress/results
- Individual/team development: learning opportunities, training, new challenges, added responsibility
- Praise, recognition and celebration of individual *and* team achievements/progress ('catch people doing things right'!)

Teamworking

> A **team** is 'a small group of people with complementary skills who are committed to a common purpose, performance goals and approaches for which they hold themselves basically jointly accountable'. *(Katzenbach & Smith)*

Advantages of teamworking	Disadvantages of teamworking
Collective skills/knowledge/effort	Longer decision-making processes
Co-ordination of individual effort	Decisions based on group agenda
Interactive > testing decisions, generating ideas, conflict resolution etc	Requires attention to group maintenance processes > draw energy away from task
Motivation through team solidarity	Decisions riskier than individual decisions
Member satisfaction (belonging, identity, achievement, share responsibility)	Norms may restrict individual contribution, apply solidarity in negative ways
Effective team > synergy: 2 + 2 = 5	Ineffective > negative synergy 2 + 2 = 3

Team formation and development (Tuckman)

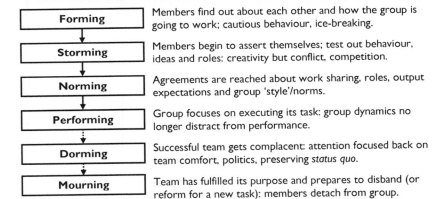

Forming — Members find out about each other and how the group is going to work; cautious behaviour, ice-breaking.

Storming — Members begin to assert themselves; test out behaviour, ideas and roles: creativity but conflict, competition.

Norming — Agreements are reached about work sharing, roles, output expectations and group 'style'/norms.

Performing — Group focuses on executing its task: group dynamics no longer distract from performance.

Dorming — Successful team gets complacent: attention focused back on team comfort, politics, preserving *status quo*.

Mourning — Team has fulfilled its purpose and prepares to disband (or reform for a new task): members detach from group.

Team diversity

- ☑ Widening range of ideas and info for decision-making, problem-solving
- ☑ Demonstrated willingness to take stakeholder views into account > commitment
- ☑ Reflect diversity of supply chain partners, customers, society
- ☑ Control risk of blinkered and complacent thinking; encourage learning, innovation
- ☑ Create group climate in which differences and ideas are welcomed and supported

Team leadership role

- ☐ Team leader role may be designated, rotated or distributed among members
- ☐ Team may be undirected/leaderless (eg T-groups) to observe/feedback processes
- ☐ **Solo leader** (autocratic, directive) v **team leader** (democratic, transformational)

Team member roles (Belbin)

Effective teamworking requires a mix and balance of **process roles**, supporting task processes *and* team maintenance processes. (NB not just job/*content* roles)

- ❏ **Plant**　　　　　　　　　Presents new ideas and solutions
- ❏ **Resource investigator**　Explores new opportunities and contacts
- ❏ **Co-ordinator**　　　　　Clarifies goals, promotes decision-making, delegates
- ❏ **Shaper**　　　　　　　　Contributes drive and inspiration
- ❏ **Monitor evaluator**　　Objectively assesses options
- ❏ **Team worker**　　　　　Listens, builds, resolves conflict
- ❏ **Implementer**　　　　　Turns ideas into practical actions
- ❏ **Completer/finisher**　　Searches out errors/omissions, ensures on-time delivery
- ❏ **Specialist**　　　　　　Provides knowledge and skills required for the task

Team processes

Cohesion
Created by: team identity, solidarity, shared goals, inter-group competition, crisis and positive leadership.

- ☑ Commitment, mutual accountability, cooperation > high performance
- ☒ Groupthink: blinkered to outside info, feedback; no questioning/dissent > poor/ risky decisions
- \> Encourage self-criticism, feedback, disagreement

Team processes and dynamics

Communication

Mature team, > less leader-centred, more inclusive and multi-directional.

Where effective:

- ❏ Open, honest, able to deal with conflicts
- ❏ Task-relevant information sharing
- ❏ All-member participation (no status barriers)
- ❏ Positive contribution styles outweigh negative

Decision-making
By leader authority, influence, majority rule (eg vote) or consensus (work towards agreement). Mature team, > less leader-centred.

Group decisions:

- ☑ Better evaluated
- ☑ More representative
- ☒ Risky-shift > more risky decisions than individual

Effective and ineffective team working

Key team values	Possible reasons for poor teamwork
Trust	Lack of support/info/resource from management
Fairness	Unclear or unrealistic individual/team objectives/expectations
Equal opportunity	Inappropriate size or composition (lack of mix/balance in roles)
Diversity	Conflicts of interest, hostility or status blocking development
Mutual respect	Under-performing individuals holding back the team
Ethical conduct	Poor leadership > politics, lack of guidance for team processes
(NB: leadership...)	Group norms negative (eg restricting output, resisting leader)

NB: This is only an overview: work carefully through Chapter 6 of your Course Book.

Conflict is constructive when it:	Conflict is destructive when it:
Introduces different solutions/options	Distracts attention from the task
Clarifies power relationships	Polarises views and 'dislocates' the group
Encourages testing of ideas	Subverts objectives > secondary agendas
Brings emotions out into the open	Fosters defensive or spoiling behaviour
Releases suppressed hostility	Creates win-lose conflicts or hostility
Prevents 'groupthink' (risky cohesion)	Results in group disintegration

- ☑ Recognise the inevitability (even necessity) of conflict in organisations
- ☑ Explicitly encourage opposition and challenge to ideas and *status quo*
- ☑ Stimulate conflict/competition/questioning as well as resolving it when necessary
- ☑ Treat the management of conflict as a major responsibility of all managers

Causes of conflict

Underlying causes	Inter-group conflict	Conflict in the team
• **Interdependence** (linked goals) and shared resources > frustration	• Institutionalised (eg trade unions v management)	• Disagreement about goals, values, priorities
• **Differences** (in goals, values and perceptions) > misunderstanding/clash	• Hierarchy based (for authority or status)	• Lack of direction/clarity
	• Functional (goal clash, resource competition)	• Poor communication
• **Authority imbalances** > competition, politics		• Limited resources (space, rewards, equipment etc)
	• Line/staff (for influence)	
• **Ambiguity** (of authority, roles, motives) > mistrust, clashes	• Resource based (over finance, staff, space etc)	• Interpersonal issues (personality clashes, unequal treatment etc)
	• Political (jockeying for power and influence)	• Hygiene issues (conditions, pay etc).

Managerial strategies for managing causes of conflict

- ❑ **Problem-solving:** bring parties together to discuss issues
- ❑ **Superordinate goals:** encourage parties to see the bigger picture, shared goals
- ❑ **Expansion of resources:** free/mobilise resources to meet both parties' needs
- ❑ **Authoritative command:** make decisive judgements to resolve issues, competition
- ❑ **Alter the human variable:** change attitudes, beliefs or perceptions underlying the conflict; take one of the conflicting parties out of the picture
- ❑ **Alter the structural variable:** re-organise work; minimise artificial status barriers and power imbalances; clarify goals/responsibilities; improve communication mechanisms; solve hygiene issues to resolve or minimise potential for conflict

Conflict management	Conflict resolution
Creating conditions in which people can interact co-operatively, and potential conflict issues discussed openly > mutual understanding and respect.	Resolving disputes or conflicts once they emerge: rules of conduct; liaison officers; confrontation/negotiation meetings; mechanisms for mediation/arbitration etc.

Equality and diversity

Equality is the principle that people should be treated fairly and without discrimination in accessing rights and benefits, compared to other groups.

Diversity is the principle that individual differences should be valued and respected, and that an organisation's workforce should broadly reflect that of its external labour market, customer base or society as a whole.

- ☑ Widening the recruitment pool: access to more skills
- ☑ Performance benefits: drawing on full contribution of people
- ☑ Reflecting diversity of external stakeholders > better relationships
- ☑ Enhanced customer satisfaction and loyalty (among diversity-sensitive consumers)
- ☑ Compliance with relevant legislation and regulation
- ☑ Enhanced flexibility and learning, through openness to difference
- ☑ Avoid: inability to target market segments; reputational damage; reduced staff contribution; inability to attract/retain talent; impoverished culture; legal costs

- ☒ Burdens and costs of formulating and administering diversity policy/practice
- ☒ Difficulties of managing/communicating effectively in ethnically diverse teams
- ☒ Difficulties and costs of managing diverse family responsibilities (flexible working etc)
- ☒ Development issues of differing educational standards and pathways
- ☒ Potential for misunderstanding, miscommunication and conflict from differences

[NB: argument for better management – *not* avoidance of diversity!]

Equal opportunity

Equal opportunity is non-discrimination in access to employment opportunities and benefits.

In the UK it is illegal to discriminate on the grounds of:

- ❑ **Sex**, marital status (Sex Discrimination Act) and (more recently) sexual orientation and sex change; and related issues (eg pregnancy, maternity and sexual harassment)
- ❑ **Race**, colour, ethnicity (Race Relations Act) and (more recently) religion and belief
- ❑ **Disability** (Disability Discrimination Act 1995): new obligation to adjust workplace to accommodate needs of disabled persons
- ❑ **Age** (Employment Equality [Age] Regulations 2006): removal of direct or implied age restrictions in recruitment and training; removal of upper age limits for unfair dismissal and redundancy; access to help and guidance; justification of compulsory early retirement; 'right to request' working beyond retirement age.

Obligation not to discriminate applies to all aspects of employment: job advertising, recruitment and selection procedures; access to training and promotion; terms and conditions of work; access to benefits; disciplinary procedures; selection for redundancy; and compulsory retirement ages.

Equal Pay Act (amended): woman's right to claim equal pay and conditions for work of equal 'value' (as measured by job evaluation) – no longer has to be 'similar work'.

Managing diversity

Wider concept than 'equal opportunity': recognises that dimensions of difference eg sex, race, age are relatively crude and obvious – and largely irrelevant to job.

- ❑ Support tolerance of individual differences – and celebrate strengths/synergy!
- ❑ Design reward systems for diverse needs/goals (eg flexible benefits)
- ❑ Design development for diverse education paths, qualifications, learning styles
- ❑ Adjust work arrangements for diverse family responsibilities
- ❑ Adjust work arrangements/environments for disabilities, age differences
- ❑ Enhance employee communications

Developing diversity/equal opportunities policy

Analyse the business environment	Check how far organisation reflects its labour/market base
Define diversity and its benefits	Business case for diversity: see p 28
Appoint diversity champions	Secure senior management support; put issues high on corporate agenda
Draft policy and codes of practice	Use a representative working party if possible
Communicate and promote the policy	Involve staff at all levels: diversity handbook, awareness training, forums, mentoring, training etc
Support via HR processes	Diversity selection/appraisal/reward criteria, training/coaching etc.
Monitor and benchmark performance	Diversity score card, employee surveys, statutory reporting etc.

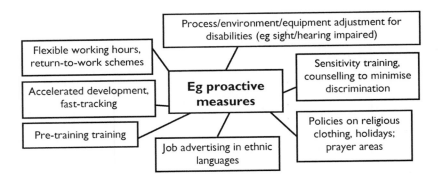

Process/environment/equipment adjustment for disabilities (eg sight/hearing impaired)

Flexible working hours, return-to-work schemes

Accelerated development, fast-tracking

Pre-training training

Eg proactive measures

Sensitivity training, counselling to minimise discrimination

Policies on religious clothing, holidays; prayer areas

Job advertising in ethnic languages

Why develop people?

For trainees:

☑ Enhanced skills/competence > self-esteem, achievement and reward potential
☑ Opportunities for career development and potentially job satisfaction
☑ Opportunities for personal development, enhanced employability

For the organisation:

☑ Enhanced skills/competence/ethics > better performance, commitment, contribution
☑ Enhanced versatility and flexibility > more efficient utilisation, adaptability to change
☑ Reduced accidents, errors/wastage and other consequences of poor performance
☑ Less need for supervision, freeing management for proactive roles (or delayering)
☑ Enhanced employer brand (eg as Investors in People) to attract quality labour
☑ Support for continuous learning, innovation, improvement > competitive advantage

Development is a **strategic activity:** directed at building and sustaining long-term competitive advantage or service improvement.

Development is a **cultural value:** a learning organisation *(Pedler et al)* 'facilitates the acquisition and sharing of knowledge, and the learning of all its members, in order continuously and strategically to transform itself in response to a rapidly changing and uncertain environment'.

Systematic approach to training

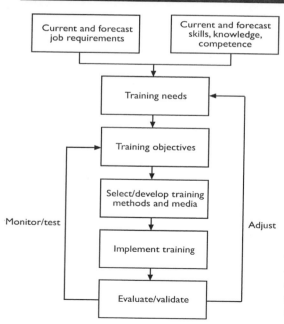

Formal **training needs analysis** may be carried out for the function, job or individual.

Training **methods/media**:

- **On-the-job**: job instruction, coaching, job rotation, assistant positions, projects

- **Off-the-job**: classes, case studies, role plays, distance learning, site visits, computer-based and e-learning, blended learning, action learning

- **Informal**: self-reflection, opportunistic coaching by manager, feedback etc.

Training may be **evaluated** for: trainee satisfaction, learning outcomes, job performance, and wider impacts (eg on results, culture).

Training needs analysis

Measure what staff need to be able to do:	Measure what staff can do:
• Job/role/competence analysis • Job descriptions, person specifications • Future plans of organisation/unit	• Observation, work sampling • Self-assessment, attitude surveys • Formal appraisal, feedback

Identify 'gap' as potential need for training/learning:
• What other interventions (eg counselling, discipline, problem-solving) may be more appropriate?
• What type of training would be most appropriate for this skill gap and these trainees?

Functional level: eg on restructuring, change of policy, new systems

Job level: eg groups of new staff, new jobs created, or updating of job descriptions

Individual level: ongoing appraisal, feedback, improvement/development planning

Training methods and media

Methods	Advantages	Disadvantages
On-the-job methods		
Sitting with Nellie	Learning in context Immediate feedback/adjustment Establishes relationships + skills	Only effective as 'Nellie' Transfers work culture (not always best practice)
Coaching	Flexible to trainee pace/needs Involves trainee in problem-solving Learning connected to job context	Requires coaching skills
Mentoring	Flexibly adjusted to trainee needs Encourages self-development Longer-term, wider development	Requires mentoring time and skills
Rotating/shadowing	Trainees experience responsibility with controlled risk May increase job satisfaction Aids management succession	May be perceived as not 'real' work May be perceived as 'nuisance' by full-timers
Action learning	Builds relationships Addresses real work problems Builds learning, problem-solving and interpersonal skills	Requires skilled facilitation

NB: this is just a brief survey: work carefully through Chapter 8 of your Course Book. You should be able to explain each of the methods mentioned...

Methods	Advantages	Disadvantages
Off-the-job methods		
Lectures/taught classes	Suits theorist/reflector styles and theory/principle-based subjects Suits large numbers of trainees	Doesn't suit hands-on Difficult learning passively Relative inflexibility
Case studies, role plays, simulations	Experimentation without risk Active problem-solving, participation	May not transfer to real job Euphoria of training may cause anticlimax at work
Open/distance learning	Economical, especially, where trainees geographically dispersed Flexible for learner pace, needs, circumstances	Only as effective as materials/programme May not suit activists/pragmatists
Visits and tours	Aids generalisation/application Raises awareness of big picture	Limited depth of content Limited flexibility
E-learning	Economical where hardware/software available Flexible to trainee pace, needs Standardised training	Technology may alienate non-expert users May not transfer to real job context
Blended learning	Best of e-learning + face-to-face Suits variety of learning styles Economical use of resources	Only as effective as programme…

Training and development

Training is 'a planned process to modify attitude, knowledge or skill behaviour through learning experiences, to achieve effective performance in any activity or range of activities'. *(Manpower Services Commission)*

Development is the wider process of growing people's knowledge and capabilities to help them in coping with change, and increasingly fulfilling their potential.

Development includes activities for:
- Gaining experience of different levels/functions/sites
- Receiving guidance, support and counselling to formulate personal/career goals
- Gaining access to learning experiences to develop skills and knowledge
- Facilitating career planning and management succession within the organisation
- Continuously updating professional skills/knowledge/standards (CPD)

Evaluating training and development activity

Level	Measurement
Trainee reaction	Feedback forms, attitude surveys: was training satisfying/useful etc?
Learning	Post-training observation, testing: did training meet objectives?
Job behaviour	Observation, work sampling: has learning been transferred to job?
Performance	Performance measures: did training impact on results, culture etc?

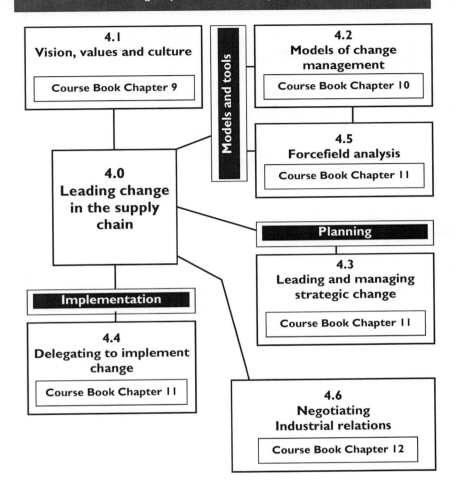

Vision

Vision is 'strategic intent, or the desired future state of the organisation… an aspiration around which a strategist… might seek to focus the attention and energies of members of the organisation'. (*Johnson & Scholes*)

☑ Overarching sense of meaning/direction > supports change/innovation
☑ Allows clarity in communication of strategic intent to business units and stakeholders
☑ Offers control and coherence (focus) by creating direction and simple rules for action
☑ Highly flexible: leaves room for diversity, exploration of options
☑ Focuses energy/attention on the future

Building a compelling vision *(meaningful; shared; influential)*

Step 1	Assess the context: stakeholders, competitors etc
Step 2	Look for trends: future needs/influences
Step 3	Think big
Step 4	Think long term
Step 5	Envision: picture desired future state vividly and in detail
Step 6	Check for passion: adjust vision until it is meaningful, exciting
Step 7	Assess resource requirements
Step 8	Invite others in
Step 9	Balance convictions with openness
Step 10	Stay objective: gather feedback, learn and adjust if necessary

---

Strategic alignment

All-embracing → **Mission** → *stimulates*

Mission statement describes purpose, business area and key values, in qualitative terms.

General → **Goals** → *stimulates*

Goals: desired future state ('where we want to get to').

Specific → **Objectives** → *stimulates*

Objectives: specific targets to pursue ('what we need to do to get there').

Detailed targets → **Strategy** → *stimulates*

Strategic plans apply to whole organisation, focusing on the broad direction over long term (3–5 years).

Implementation targets → **Tactics** → *stimulates*

Tactical plans apply to particular divisions and functions, focusing on tasks required to pursue strategies in particular markets, over medium term (1–2 years).

Action targets → **Operational plans**

Operational plans apply to departments and units, focusing on detailed activity, targets, resources, over short term (up to 1 year).

- **Vertical alignment:** ensure that all sub-unit efforts contribute to overall corporate mission, for unity of direction.

- **Horizontal alignment:** ensure that efforts of different sub-units dovetail with each other, for co-ordinated effort and a coherent face to the world.

34

- ☑ Cohesive, shared view of direction and purpose
- ☑ Prevents duplication of effort and resources: encourages co-operation
- ☑ Gives each team a sense of corporate impact: role within bigger picture
- ☑ Improved planning/understanding, prioritisation
- ☑ Improved measurement of individual unit value: tied to business justification

Securing stakeholder buy-in　　*(Kotter & Schlesinger)*

PARTICIPATION	☑ People more likely to support changes
	☑ Better quality change plans with employee input
	☒ Can be a lengthy process, if consensus sought
	☒ Requires strong relationship of trust

EDUCATION AND COMMUNICATION	☑ Can persuade people to internalise change
	☑ Greater trust from perception of openness
	☑ Gives some sense of control (reduced insecurity)
	☒ May be time-consuming

FACILITATION AND SUPPORT	☑ Reduces fear of loss of competence/security
	☑ Demonstrates management commitment
	☑ Furthers implementation of change (eg via training)
	☒ May be time-consuming and costly

POWER/COERCION	☑ Effective in authoritarian cultures; situations of crisis change; where stakeholders have little power
	☒ At best, secures compliance (not commitment)
	☒ Fails to address resistance: may re-emerge later
	☒ Makes employees feel powerless > low morale

NEGOTIATION	☑ Resistance is systematically confronted
	☑ Win-win may enhance decision and commitment
	☒ Can polarise positions > adversarial

Corporate social responsibility

CSR promotes the integration of stakeholder issues into business operations... treating stakeholders ethically or in a responsible manner... to produce an overall positive impact on society. *(CIPS)*

Upstream activity: eg wages/conditions of low-cost supplier

↓

Purchasing firm: eg ethical trading/ employment, corporate governance, business and professional ethics

↓

Downstream activity: eg consumer rights, product disposal/recycle

CIPS key principles of CSR
- ❑ Environmental responsibility
- ❑ Human rights
- ❑ Equality and diversity
- ❑ Corporate governance
- ❑ Sustainability
- ❑ Impact on society
- ❑ Ethics and ethical trading
- ❑ Biodiversity

Why CSR?

'Social responsibility of business = profit maximisation'>> **'enlightened self-interest'**.

- **Compliance** with law, regulation and codes of practice
- **Financial/operational** incentives and penalties (eg 'polluter pays' taxes)
- **Sustainability**: social wellbeing minimises risks of instability; conservation of resources preserves viability; ethical trading preserves business relationships
- **Market demand**: ability to attract/retain customers
- **Employer/corporate brand**: ability to attract/retain labour and chain partners, sustain brand equity (reputation capital), media profile

Ethics are a set of moral principles or values about what constitutes 'right' and 'wrong' behaviour.

Macro issues	Corporate issues	Individual issues
Business in society; globalisation, labour exploitation, impacts on environment	Interaction with stakeholders: ethical trading, employment, sourcing > CSR	Individual conduct: integrity, confidentiality, professional competence etc

Compliance based approach	Integrity based approach
Rules/procedures ensure that firm complies with relevant law/regulation > prevention and disciplining of violations	Education/communication/culture focuses on ethical values and shared responsibility for resolving ethical issues

Purchasing contribution to ethical/CSR objectives:
- ❑ Draw up and enforce codes of practice for ethical sourcing
- ❑ Adhere to CIPS ethical code and Ethical Trading Initiative principles
- ❑ Encourage/enforce ethical employment/environmental practices in suppliers
- ❑ Adhere to health and safety, equal opportunity and ethical employment practices

Organisational culture

Culture is 'the collective programming of the mind which distinguishes the members of one category of people from another'. *(Hofstede)*

Organisational culture is 'a pattern of beliefs and expectations shared by the organisation's members, which produce norms which powerfully shape the behaviour of individuals and groups in the organisation' *(Schwartz & Davies)*. In other words: 'the way we do things around here'!

Influences on organisation culture:
- ❑ History/development
- ❑ Environment (nation, region, industry)
- ❑ Individuals and groups
- ❑ Management and leadership
- ❑ HR systems (reinforcing desired norms, values)

Outward expressions
(norms, artefacts, rituals)
Values and beliefs
Underlying assumptions

Cultural web (*Johnson & Scholes*):

- 'the taken-for-granted assumptions, or **paradigm**, of an organisation,

- and the **behavioural manifestations** of organisational culture'.

Can be used to analyse the culture of any organisation (by listing examples of each factor in the appropriate circle).

[Mnemonic: **PS CROPS**?]

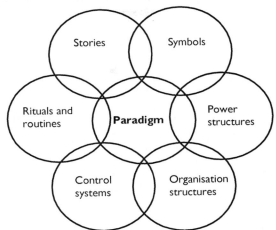

Harrison's model of cultural types

Power culture	Power centred in a key figure/leader; control via personal communication; little formalisation, rules, procedures.
Role culture	Classical organisation (bureaucracy); formalised, impersonal: authority based on position, function; conformity to rules and procedures.
Task culture	Management focus > outputs/results; team-based, flexible, horizontal; values expertise, info-sharing and collaboration (eg project management).
Person culture	Serves interests of individuals: eg barristers in chambers, consultants. Management = administrative support function (rather than directive).

Deal and Kennedy's model of cultural types

	High risk	
Slow feedback	BET-YOUR-COMPANY *culture* ('slow and steady wins the race')	HARD 'MACHO' *culture* ('find a mountain and climb it')
	PROCESS *culture* ('it's not what you do, it's the way that you do it')	WORK HARD/PLAY HARD *culture* ('find a need and fill it')
	Low risk	**Fast feedback**

Work carefully through Chapter 9 of your Course Book, if you need more detail!

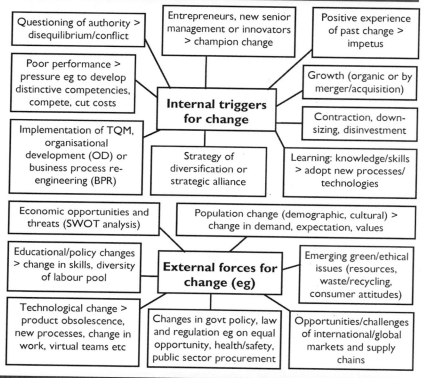

Questioning of authority > disequilibrium/conflict

Entrepreneurs, new senior management or innovators > champion change

Positive experience of past change > impetus

Poor performance > pressure eg to develop distinctive competencies, compete, cut costs

Growth (organic or by merger/acquisition)

Internal triggers for change

Contraction, down-sizing, disinvestment

Implementation of TQM, organisational development (OD) or business process re-engineering (BPR)

Strategy of diversification or strategic alliance

Learning: knowledge/skills > adopt new processes/ technologies

Economic opportunities and threats (SWOT analysis)

Population change (demographic, cultural) > change in demand, expectation, values

Educational/policy changes > change in skills, diversity of labour pool

External forces for change (eg)

Emerging green/ethical issues (resources, waste/recycling, consumer attitudes)

Technological change > product obsolescence, new processes, change in work, virtual teams etc

Changes in govt policy, law and regulation eg on equal opportunity, health/safety, public sector procurement

Opportunities/challenges of international/global markets and supply chains

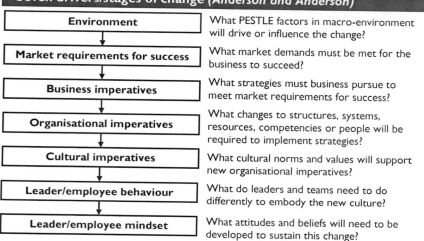

Seven drivers/stages of change *(Anderson and Anderson)*

Environment	What PESTLE factors in macro-environment will drive or influence the change?
Market requirements for success	What market demands must be met for the business to succeed?
Business imperatives	What strategies must business pursue to meet market requirements for success?
Organisational imperatives	What changes to structures, systems, resources, competencies or people will be required to implement strategies?
Cultural imperatives	What cultural norms and values will support new organisational imperatives?
Leader/employee behaviour	What do leaders and teams need to do differently to embody the new culture?
Leader/employee mindset	What attitudes and beliefs will need to be developed to sustain this change?

Forcefield analysis

- **Driving forces** (pushing towards a preferred state: *for* change)
- **Restraining forces** (pushing back towards the way things are: *for the status quo*)

Interplay of forces determines current state of the organisation *and* pace and direction of change at any given moment. Map for analysis:

Introduction of performance review

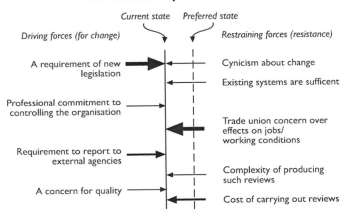

Formulate strategies to:

- ❏ Weaken or eliminate restraining forces
- ❏ Strengthen driving forces or add new driving forces

Organisational development

Organisational development (OD) is 'an effort (1) planned, (2) organisation-wide, and (3) managed from the top, to (4) increase organisation development and health through (5) planned interventions in the organisation's processes, using behavioural science knowledge.' (*Beckhard*)

- ❏ Focus on individual/social behaviour: culture, commitment, conflict, change etc
- ❏ Strategic, proactive, systematic process > long-term behavioural changes
- ❏ Aim > individual development, quality of working life, organisational effectiveness
- ❏ Key values: mutual respect, open communication, trust, commitment, collaboration, value of personal growth at work etc

Planned change approach	Action research approach
Diagnosis > planning > action > stabilisation > termination	Act > observe/measure > analyse > plan/adjust > monitor/feedback > act etc
(n step)	**(cyclical)**

Planned change: the three-stage model (Lewin/Schein)

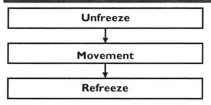

Unfreeze	Disrupt existing equilibrium Facilitate 'unlearning' of old ways
Movement	Introduce imbalances so that driving forces outweigh restraining forces
Refreeze	Consolidate and reinforce new equilibrium

(**NB**: in fast-changing environments, 'freezing' is seen as counter-productive. Organisation may want to maintain constant 'unfrozen'/adaptable mindset, without 'rehardening'.)

Eight-step model for major change (Kotter)	
Step 1	Establish a sense of urgency (need for change)
Step 2	Form a guiding coalition (to drive change)
Step 3	Create a vision for change
Step 4	Communicate the vision
Step 5	Empower people to act on the vision (eg training, resources, authority)
Step 6	Create 'short-term wins' (celebrate milestones to energise/encourage)
Step 7	Consolidate improvements to produce further change
Step 8	Institutionalise new approaches (embed in culture, procedures, systems)

Using external change agents

- ☑ More likely to be objective, dispassionate, non-political + represent stakeholder views
- ☑ Better able to question/challenge *status quo*; more open responses from staff
- ☑ May have technical expertise in research and OD interventions
- ☑ Dedicated to change programme
- ☑ Signal significant/focused investment in change

- ☒ May raise suspicion: 'ivory tower' approach, doing management's 'dirty work' etc
- ☒ May lack insight into particular industry/culture etc of organisation
- ☒ Cost/time of exercise

Stakeholder consultation and engagement

 Consultation is the process of exchanging information with stakeholders as part of the change process. **Engagement** is the process of securing their interest, collaboration and support for the change programme.

Aims:
- Allow the views and needs of stakeholders to be taken into account
- Develop change objectives/processes that are likely to be supported/accepted
- Ensure accountability for change decisions which affect stakeholders (public sector)
- Enhance quality of change plans through input from expert/involved stakeholders
- Provide for issues management: pre-empt conflict or negative PR
- Provide for crisis management: dealing with negative contingencies/impacts positively

Mechanisms:
- Existing steering groups, task forces, committees, cross-functional teams
- Temporary advisory or task-force teams
- Consultation programmes for key stakeholder groups
- Issuing proposals and inviting responses: eg via public advertisement, direct contact, workshops, meetings or public forums
- Unveiling proposals at stakeholder meetings or seminars

See also >> Unit 2.1, 2.3

Change leadership styles (Dunphy and Stace)

- ☐ **Coercion:** senior management imposes changes
- ☐ **Direction:** managers use authority to make decisions re future, changes
- ☐ **Consultation:** employees are given limited involvement in setting change goals
- ☐ **Collaboration:** widespread employee involvement in decisions about the future

	Incremental change	Transformative change
Collaborative/ Consultative style	*Participative evolution strategy* Use when: • Minor adjustments required • Time for participation • Key interest groups favour change	*Charismatic transformation strategy* Use when: • Major adjustments required • Little time for participation • There is support for radical change
Directive/ Coercive style	*Forced evolution strategy* Use when: • Minor adjustments required • Time for participation BUT • Key interest groups oppose change	*Dictatorial transformation strategy* Use when: • Major adjustments required • No time for participation • No internal support BUT • Change necessary for survival

See also >> Unit 4.1 (Education/communication, facilitation/support, negotiation, coercion etc)

Resolving conflict with stakeholders

Thomas-Kilmann instrument:

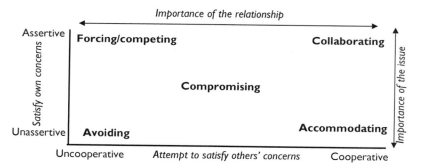

- **Avoiding**: you withdraw from conflict or attempt to sweep under the carpet

  - ☑ Avoids immediate tensions; allows 'cooling off' period or referral to others
  - ☒ Underlying problems don't get resolved > frustration, later emergence

- **Forcing/competing**: you impose your solution on the problem

  - ☑ You get your way, win on an important issue, break down others' inflexibility
  - ☒ The other person is likely to feel defeated > damage ongoing relationship

- **Accommodating**: you concede the issue without a fight, to preserve harmony

  - ☑ Avoids upsetting people, preserves relationship
  - ☒ Your authority is undermined, you 'lose' on an issue that may be worth winning

- **Compromising**: you bargain/negotiate, so each party trades concessions for gains

  - ☑ Reaches agreement both parties can live with, enabling you to get back to work
  - ☒ Solution is often more expedient than truly effective/satisfying

- **Collaborating**: both parties work to find a 'win-win' to clearly stated needs

  - ☑ Respects both positions, facilitates trust and learning, generates creative options and ensures both parties are satisfied by and committed to the result
  - ☒ Not always possible in time available

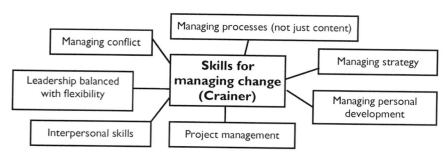

CHANGE	v	**TRANSFORMATION**
(Gradual, incremental, small-step)		*(Fundamental level, significant scale)*

Evolutionary change	Revolutionary change
Often a proactive approach	Often a reactive approach
Builds on *status quo* in small steps over a long period of time	Seeks to overthrow *status quo* over a relatively short period of time
Basis of improvement strategies eg *kaizen* (continuous improvement) and total quality management (TQM)	Basis of improvement strategies eg business process re-engineering (BPR): heavy investment > transformative improvement
Requires only realistic, small, operational changes > 'bottom up' implementation (via suggestion schemes, quality circles, self-improvement plans etc)	Requires discontinuous, sweeping change across existing structures/systems: can only be implemented from the 'top down' by strong vision, leadership from management
Effective for building up organisational learning and competencies > response to ongoing patterns of gradual change. **eg** customer demand, sector dynamics, cultural change	Effective where *status quo* dysfunctional. Response to 'disruptive' change, crisis, need for new paradigms: **eg** new technology, process realignment due to competitive pressure, restructure for merger

Sample fundamental change strategy: BPR

Business process re-engineering (BPR) is 'the fundamental rethinking and radical redesign of business processes to achieve dramatic improvement in critical, contemporary measures of performance, such as cost, quality, service and speed.' *(Hammer & Champy)*

- **'Discontinuous thinking'**: breaking away from old rules and assumptions > clean slate for radical change.

- **Strategic approach**: must be supported and driven by a strategic plan and support of top management.

Sample incremental change strategy: kaizen

Kaizen is the Japanese term for continuous improvement. 'It is both a rigorous, scientific method of using statistical quality control and an adaptive framework of organisational values and beliefs that keep management and workers alike focused on zero defects'.

- **Kaizen**: continuous improvement by incremental (small step) improvements.

Plan	Implement (small scale)	Measure	Evaluate results/process > identify learning

- **Hansei kaizen:** continuous improvement through rigorous self-reflection: constant monitoring, questioning and feedback-seeking > open to areas for improvement.

- **Kaizen teian** ('proposal'): involving all employees as collaborators in continuous improvement: eg cross-functional kaizen teams work together to plan and implement incremental improvement projects.

Change objectives and targets

Planned change (project management) model: 'change can be broken down into smaller tasks, and these can be done in some preferred, if overlapping sequence'. *(Boddy)* BUT uncertain outcomes/goals, unclear tactics/sub-tasks and time estimates >

Emergent change model: 'some thinking ahead of time' + 'some adaptation *en route*' *(Mintzberg)*. Fluid, adaptive and/or logical-incremental (short-range, small-step plans).

SMARTER CHANGE OBJECTIVES:	
Specific	Precisely stated outcomes/deliverables
Measurable	Targets for which quantified info is available
Attainable	Realistically achievable (if challenging) with available resources
Relevant	Aligned with strategic objectives of organisation and unit
Time-bounded	Given a clear, realistic deadline or timescale for achievement
Evaluated	Assessed as worth pursuing: cost/benefit analysis
Responsible	Taking into account impacts on stakeholders in light of CSR goals

Delegation

Delegation is the process through which a superior hands over to a subordinate (or team) part of his or her own authority to make decisions or take actions. (It is also a style of leadership in Hersey and Blanchard's situational model of leadership: >> Unit 1.3)

Advantages of delegation	Reasons for reluctance to delegate
Recognises limits to manager workload	Low confidence in staff (possibly justified)
Frees managers to focus on higher roles	Pressure of accountability > retain control
Results enhanced by input from lower levels (with expertise, detailed info, front-line contact)	Lack of skills in time management (eg to see need for delegation) or delegation (eg tendency to over-control)
Development opportunities for staff	Perceived threat of role being undermined
Aids promotion/succession planning	Desire for familiar, routine workload
Contributes to staff job satisfaction	Organisation culture resistant to delegation

When to delegate

☑ Trust can be placed in the competence and reliability of subordinates *and*
☑ Work to be delegated is routine, repetitive or of low consequence *or*
☑ The quality of the work/decision will be improved by subordinate involvement *or*
☑ Subordinate acceptance and commitment is important for effective implementation

Best suited to high-readiness (able and willing and/or confident) teams *(Hersey/Blanchard)*

How to delegate

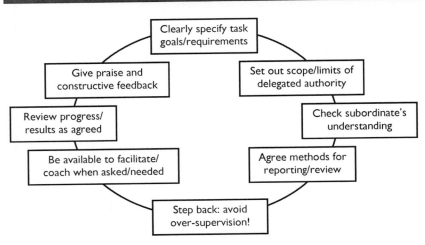

Forcefield analysis

- **Driving forces** (pushing towards a preferred state: *for* change)
- **Restraining forces** (pushing back towards the way things are: *for* the *status quo*)

>> *Unit 4.2*

Individual responses to change

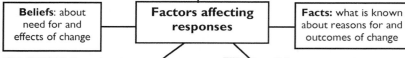

Impacts of change on the individual: physical (eg different shift patterns); circumstantial (eg relocation); social (eg new teams); psychological (eg requirement to learn new skills: disorientation); +ve or –ve.

Beliefs: about need for and effects of change

Factors affecting responses

Facts: what is known about reasons for and outcomes of change

Feelings: emotions about the process or outcomes eg fear, pride, excitement

Values: +ve and –ve moral judgements re process or outcomes

The coping cycle

Model of human coping with grief and loss (*Elizabeth Kubler-Ross*) applied to change.

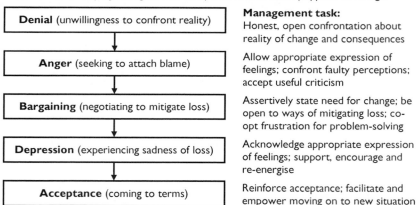

Denial (unwillingness to confront reality)

Anger (seeking to attach blame)

Bargaining (negotiating to mitigate loss)

Depression (experiencing sadness of loss)

Acceptance (coming to terms)

Management task:
Honest, open confrontation about reality of change and consequences

Allow appropriate expression of feelings; confront faulty perceptions; accept useful criticism

Assertively state need for change; be open to ways of mitigating loss; co-opt frustration for problem-solving

Acknowledge appropriate expression of feelings; support, encourage and re-energise

Reinforce acceptance; facilitate and empower moving on to new situation

Listen, empathise and acknowledge feelings but:
>> **reframe** with positive perspective, support, encouragement, resources to cope
>> **co-opt** energy of anger/frustration for constructive criticism, problem-solving

Causes of resistance to change (Bedeian)

- ❏ **Parochial self-interest**: vested interest in maintaining *status quo* eg perceived threats to: established ways of working (and worker competence); social arrangements and relationships; health, safety and well-being; earnings/livelihood.

- ❏ **Misunderstanding and lack of trust**: people do not understand reason/purpose of change, and mistrust management's intentions. May be aggravated where change is *imposed* (without consultation/information).

- ❏ **Contradictory assessments**: people have a different perception of the need for (and consequences of) change than is being conveyed by management. (NB: Can lead to constructive criticism and improved proposals for change.)

- ❏ **Low tolerance of change**: insecurity and dislike of change/uncertainty: fear of inability to cope; overwhelm (multiple large-scale changes); exhaustion (constant change); cultural resistance (eg in bureaucracies).

Organisational barriers to change

Barrier	Mitigating action
Focus on internal processes, efficiency and stability	Focus on customer, service quality or innovation: compelling vision
Bureaucracy: vertical barriers, 'silos', formality, hierarchy, rules, conformity culture > rigidity	Encourage cross-functional partnership and network structures; emphasise project/task groups; break down status barriers; challenge rules; reward creativity, questioning, learning
Power and politics: red tape, hoarding information, competition	Devolve responsibility, share/expand power; replace red tape with goals/values; emphasise collaboration; minimise status differentials; clarify role boundaries
Security-seeking, risk aversion > analysis paralysis, strategic rigidity	Use adaptive/emergent/incremental strategy approaches; encourage/reward risk taking and learning (within acceptable bounds)
Deference culture	Encourage input/challenge/questioning; recognise contribution at all levels; remove status differentials
Blame culture	Praise instead of blame; look for people 'doing something right'; encourage mutual accountability; allow mistakes as learning opportunities
Limited resources	Introduce changes incrementally; encourage long-term view of return on change investment

Why change programmes fail

Ritualisation of change	Continual incremental change programmes come to be seen as empty rituals, rather than meaningful changes
Hijacked processes	Leaders or units hijack change efforts in order to serve their own agendas (eg downsizing, power enhancement)
Erosion	The programme is overtaken by other events and priorities emerging in the organisation: momentum is lost or diverted
Reinvention	The attempted change is reinterpreted through the lens of the old culture, which simply reinforces the *status quo* ('we're already doing that')
Ivory tower change	Change driven by senior or external agents is perceived to be out of touch with the realities of the market, losing credibility
Inattention to symbols	Change agents fail to link the 'big messages' about change to organisational values and symbols. Change may be seen as irrelevant – or the wrong message (eg blame) may be given.
Uncontrolled/ uncoordinated effort	New practices are inconsistent with the thrust of change as understood by people in the organisation, creating lack of coherence
Behavioural compliance	People comply with changes, without commitment: the programme may look successful, but the changes may not be effective or lasting

Johnson & Scholes

Eight reasons for failure of change programmes (Kotter):

1 Allowing too much complexity (not breaking change down into manageable chunks)
2 Failing to build a coalition of stakeholder support
3 Lack of a clear vision for the purpose and direction of change
4 Failing to communicate the vision clearly
5 Allowing resistance and barriers to gather
6 Lack of short-terms wins in the change plan (to create momentum and confidence)
7 Stopping short (failing to consolidate changes or push for ongoing improvement)
8 Failing to embed changes in the corporate culture

For mitigating actions: see Kotter's eight-step model of major change **>> Page 40**

Negotiation is a process whereby two parties come together to confer, in a situation in which there is some conflict of interests between them, with a view to concluding a jointly acceptable agreement. It can be applied in a range of contexts, including commercial and industrial negotiations and general conflict resolution and problem solving.

The negotiation process

Pre-negotiation preparation

- Data gathering and analysis
- Stakeholder/bargaining power analysis
- Identifying key issues/priorities
- Planning strategy and tactics
- Aligning team positions
- Preparing the meeting

Negotiation/interaction

- Opening/introductions
- Presentations of each party's position
- Identifying common ground
- Exchanging concessions
- Final offer/position summary
- Agreement

Post-negotiation follow-up

- Written summary of agreement
- Gaining stakeholder acceptance
- Implementing agreed measures
- Monitoring/evaluation
- Negotiation review and learning

Pre-negotiation planning

- ❑ Gather adequate info to build negotiating position and anticipate opposing positions
- ❑ Take stakeholder needs/fears into account (> integrative approach)
- ❑ Prepare coherent, consistent approach by negotiating team
- ❑ Establish informed/agreed response to possible contingencies (best/worst case)
- ❑ Ensure team is in agreement as to minimum acceptable terms, fall-back position, items not negotiable or subject to concession etc.

Stakeholder mapping/ analysis	• Assess bargaining strengths (relative power)
	• Assess motivations (needs/fears; resistance/support)
	• Assess desired outcomes (aims, areas for concession etc)
	• *>> Unit 2.1*

Determine range of negotiation	• Determine and rank objectives as high/medium/low priority • High-priority objectives may be non-negotiable • Low-priority objectives may be tradable as concessions • Define acceptable range (between best possible and worst acceptable outcomes) for each party: overlap area is open to negotiation

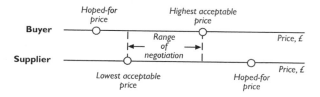

• Define 'walk-away' position: Best Alternative to Negotiated Agreement (BATNA)

Align negotiating team	• Ensure all members aligned as to strategy/tactics • Resolve conflicts of interest within the team • Trial run or rehearsal of dynamics/position

Use of teams in negotiation
- ☑ Pooling knowledge/skills/styles in negotiation
- ☑ Encourage discussion, info sharing, options generation
- ☑ Shared responsibility > less pressure, less adversarial
- ☑ Support, back up, error coverage for individuals
- ☒ Potential for poorly integrated position, tactics
- ☒ Intra-team competition > more pressure, adversarialism

Negotiation approaches

Distributive	**Integrative**
Bargaining > distribution of limited resources: 'dividing up a fixed pie' > zero-sum, win-lose or competitive outcome.	Collaborative problem-solving to increase options available ('expand the pie'): seek mutually satisfying or added-value solutions ('win-win').
• Exaggerated initial positions/demands • Polarise conflicting positions • Withholding info on common ground • Using levers to coerce, manipulate other party to make concessions • Offering minimal return concessions • Never making the first concession • Over-state own concessions	• Openness about needs/concerns • Generating options with genuine mutual or trade-off benefits • Focusing on areas of common ground • Supporting other party in accepting • Modelling flexibility re counter-offers • Using concessions to build trust (unilateral, if clearly acknowledged, relatively low-risk, justifiable: *Malhotra*)

Position-based	Principle-based *(Fisher and Ury)*
Each sides takes a 'position' and attempts to get an outcome as close to that position as possible. • Bargain hard > often elicit hard counter-response • Bargain soft (concessions) > compromise • Often relationship-damaging process	Both sides work together to attack a shared problem or maximise a shared opportunity. • Hard on problem: soft on people • Reconcile interests (needs/fears), not positions • Generate options: expand the pie • Use objectively fair standards

Industrial relations and employee relations

Industrial relations is 'all the rules, practices and conventions governing interactions between managements and their workforces, normally involving collective employee representation and bargaining'. *(Graham and Bennett)*

Employee relations is 'all those areas of HRM that involve general relationships with employees, through collective agreements where trade unions are recognised [industrial relations] and/or through commonly applied policies for employee involvement and communications.' *(Armstrong)*

Employee negotiations:

❑ **Grievance/conflict handling**: individual or collective dispute resolution. (Informal negotiation/problem-solving; mediation/arbitration processes; formal grievance procedures with mechanisms for escalation etc.)

❑ **Group problem-solving**: any conflict of interest between work groups, departments, stakeholder groups in change programmes etc.

❑ **Negotiation of terms and conditions**: individual level (eg personal contracts) or collective (agreements between employer and plant/industry/national employee representatives: **collective bargaining**).

Commercial negotiations	v	Employee negotiations
Negotiators select partners (eg selected suppliers)		Negotiating parties fixed (eg by interest groups, legal entitlement, representation)
Often conducted remotely (eg by telephone or e-mail)		Always face-to-face: higher emotional tone; greater need for adjournments and follow-up meetings
Often have BATNA: ability to 'walk away', agree to disagree		'No agreement' outcome not available: parties locked into relationship
Based on transactional, time-bounded relationships with exit strategies		Based on assumption that parties have to have an on-going, long-term relationship